DATE DUE

| | | | |
|---|---|---|---|
| | | | |
| | | | |
| | | | |
| | | | |
| | | | |
| | | | |
| | | | |
| | | | |
| | | | |
| | | | |
| | | | |
| | | | |
| | | | |
| | | | |

# The RACQUETBALL Book

*Messner Books by Margaret Poynter*

THE RACQUETBALL BOOK
THE JIMMY CARTER STORY
FRISBEE FUN

# The RACQUETBALL Book

## by Margaret Poynter

### Photos by Don Meyer and Terry Andrues
### Diagrams by Don Meyer

Julian Messner (M) New York

Copyright © 1980 by Margaret Poynter
All rights reserved including the right of
reproduction in whole or in part in any form.
Published by Julian Messner, a Simon & Schuster
Division of Gulf & Western Corporation, Simon &
Schuster Building, 1230 Avenue of the Americas,
New York, N.Y. 10020.

Manufactured in the United States of America

Design by Alex D'Amato

**Library of Congress Cataloging in Publication Data**

Poynter, Margaret.
  The racquetball book.

  SUMMARY: Introduces the game of racquetball, its
equipment, clothing, rules, techniques, and some of its
champion players.
  1. Racquetball—Juvenile literature.  [1. Racquet-
ball]  I. Meyer, Don.  II. Andrues, Terry.  III. Title.
GV1017.R3P69      796.34      79-24534
ISBN 0-671-33014-4

*To Roger,*
*who was a champion right from the start*

# ACKNOWLEDGMENTS

I owe so much to so many people. Among the ones I must thank are:

Mathew Tekulsky, for all of those great ideas

Mike Hogan of the Phillips Organisation, for the material and the photos

Laurie Brooks of the Pasadena Athletic Club, for her time and her interest

And, of course, Chris, Jennifer, Carla and Willie, for being such willing and patient models.

# TO THE READER

Racquetball is a sport for both boys and girls. So why do I use the one word "he" instead of saying "he or she" all through this book?

*I'm* a girl so it's certainly not because I don't think girls are important. And it's not because I mind writing "he or she" again and again. It's because this book would be so much harder to read with all of those extra words.

For instance, would you like to keep reading sentences like the following?

"To win in racquetball, you must hit the ball to where he or she isn't. Make him or her run, force him or her to "dig" the ball out of the corner, hit the ball high over his or her head."

It does sound awkward, doesn't it? So please understand. I'm just trying to make things easier for both you and me, and him and her.

# Contents

**Chapter**

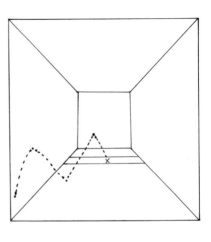

# (1)

# *Inventing A New Game*

Do you want to be the first one of your crowd to get in on a new sport? Do you want to join some popular television, movie, and sports stars in one of their favorite activities? Do you want to learn how to play a game in which you'll be able to compete with an adult and come out on top?

Then racquetball is for you. This game combines the fast pace of baseball, the skills of tennis, and the excitement of handball. The fun and exercise can be shared by almost everyone in your family. Racquetball can be played by boys and girls, and their fathers and mothers.

Racquetball has been around for only thirty years. It was developed by some tennis players who thought it would be fun to combine tennis and handball. They used tennis balls and paddle tennis racquets, and followed many of the rules of handball. Then in 1949, Joe Sobek, a tennis and squash pro, designed a shortened tennis racquet to take the place of the wooden paddle, and the game of racquetball was born.

Soon a lot of people were finding out that hitting a ball with a small racquet is a fast way to get a good, hard workout. Since a full game can be played in as little as twenty or thirty minutes, players started using the courts during their lunch hour or before breakfast.

Within ten years, the game was being played all over the United States. In 1969, some sports officials met in St. Louis, Missouri and formed the International Racquetball Association (IRA). The IRA's current address is 5545 Murray Avenue, Suite 202, Memphis, Tennessee 38104. Its purpose is to help organize and improve the game. It gives players a way to exchange news. They tell each other about tournaments, the latest equipment, and better ways to make winning shots and to keep in shape.

The first professional racquetball tournament was held in 1974. Now local, regional, national, and international tournaments are open to people of all ages and all levels of skill. In 1976, the National Junior Championships drew over 200 young players from 30 states. These boys and girls all started out the same way—just wanting to have a good time playing racquetball. They found that by practicing and developing their ability, they could become champions.

In 1970, there were only 75,000 racquetball players in this country. Today there are seven and a half million. It is thought that by 1982 there will be 29,000,000! Should *you* join them? Let's look at some of the good things about racquetball.

First, you are the one who decides how easy or how hard the game will be. You can walk onto a court right now and start playing.

However, you may find that it is too easy for you. You want more of a challenge. This book will help you learn the shots and strategy of the champions. Within just a few weeks, you'll find that you've become a good player. Within a few months, you may be entering competitions.

Racquetball can be played by third or fourth graders. It can also be played by some of their grandparents! Someone who is barely five feet tall can compete successfully with someone who is over six feet tall. Racquetball is an equalizer because there is no physical contact between opponents.

Your game can be slow and relaxing, or it can be fast and fierce. You can practice alone or with a friend. The court is small, so you short legged players can keep up with those long legs. It's enclosed so you don't have to worry about breaking a window or losing a ball.

You don't have to wait until you find a court that's available. You can practice anywhere there's a garage door or a wall in a safe area.

You can slim down your figure or develop your muscles while you have a good time. You can make friends, while releasing your excess energy.

Make racquetball the kind of game *you* want it to be. Don't push yourself unless you feel like it. However, when you're ready to go on to serious play, don't forget one important thing. Racquetball is supposed to be *fun*. Continue to enjoy yourself even if you climb up the ladder to the national finals.

$$\textbf{(2)}$$

# What Do You Need To Get Started?

You don't need a lot of money to get started in racquetball, because only two pieces of equipment are necessary: a racquet and a ball. It's even possible that you won't have to buy any balls right away. See if you can get some experienced players to give you their old ones. Many balls are thrown away when they have lost their "liveliness," and don't bounce or rebound as well as they should. Since the balls react more slowly when a beginner hits them, they'll give you more time to plan your returns. Thus, you'll be able to practice at a slower pace.

Or how about using some old tennis balls for your first practice sessions? Paint or dye them a dark color so they'll be easier to see. Tennis balls will force you to play a fast, hard hitting game, and that's good practice, too.

The regulation ball is about two inches in diameter and weighs a little less than an ounce and a half. Sports stores carry different brands such as Seamco, Ektelon, and Voit. They are all good balls, but as you try them out, you may find that you prefer one over the other. The main requirement for a racquetball is that it be "live." At room temperature, it should bounce 67 to 72 inches when it's dropped from a height of 100 inches.

You can spend as little as $5 or as much as $50 for a racquet. If your local "Y" or youth club has racquetball courts, try out a few racquets before you buy your own. Pick one with a handle that feels comfortable in your hand. To get a good grip, you shouldn't have to spread your fingers or crowd them. As you hold the racquet with your middle and fourth fingers touching your thumb, it shouldn't twist or turn when you hit the ball.

The handle of a regulation racquet can't be more than seven inches long. The length of the head can't be more than eleven inches, and the width can't be more than twenty-seven inches. This size makes it ideal for a small hand. Bigger players like it because it feels like an extension of their arm.

Nylon strings are used by almost all good players. They not only last longer and cost less than gut, but also have just the right amount of resilience, or "give". Whether you have the strings strung tightly or a little loose is up to you.

Racquet frames are made of wood, aluminum, or fiberglass. The aluminum one is the most long lasting. All types give good control of the ball, but fiberglass helps to absorb the shock of the ball when it hits the strings. This absorbency makes the game easier on your hand and arm.

As you're testing out the various racquets, notice such things as weight and length. If you're strong enough to control a longer, heavier model, get one. Most younger players will be better off with a small, light model. The short length will be more than offset by the easier control. You'll soon find out it's the player, not the equipment, that makes the difference.

All racquetball racquets have a wrist thong. Don't forget

to use it while you're playing. A racquet could easily slip out of your sweaty hand and put your opponent out of action.

Racquetball players do work up a good sweat. For this reason, you might want to wear head and wrist bands.

Some players wear a glove on their playing hand. If you do, the material should be thin enough so that you don't lose your "feel," and rough, or nubby, enough so that the racquet won't slip around in your hand.

No special clothing is necessary for racquetball. Most players wear cut-offs or shorts, and a T-shirt. The shirt is important because it will lessen the sting if a flying ball hits you. Whatever you wear should be comfortable, not too loose and floppy, and not too binding. Cotton clothing will absorb perspiration and keep you cooler than synthetic fabrics.

All clothing should be light colored. Blacks, blues, and dark greens make it hard for other players to see the exact position of the ball as it passes you. A special line of racquetball fashions is now being designed. You may eventually want to buy some of the shirts, blouses, and shorts.

Once you're sure the sport is for you, get a pair of racquetball shoes. They have the thick tread of basketball shoes, but are much lighter. This combination will give you a faster, safer game. Until you get racquetball shoes, you should wear tennis shoes with a good tread. You'll need the traction they provide.

Always wear gym socks. They will absorb perspiration and help to prevent a painful crop of blisters.

Many sports stores sell special eye guards that are held onto your head by a band. At present, most players don't use them, but *you* should. Racquetballs travel with a great deal of force and could cause a severe injury to your eye. In fact, Canada already has a law that requires racquetball players to wear eye guards, and several of our states are considering such a law. Don't wait until you're forced to wear them. Some of your friends may think they're "uncool," or "silly." But let's face it, you don't want to wear an eye patch or an artificial eye for the rest of your life.

**Keep your eyes on the ball—with eye guards.**

You should not wear eye glasses while you're playing racquetball. Get some eye guards with prescription lenses.

If someone does get hit in the eye with a ball, *stop the game and report the accident to an adult*. The eye may be all right, but only a doctor can say for certain.

Aside from eye injuries, there are only two other dangers in racquetball—falls, and being hit with the racquet. Accidents don't have to happen. If the court floor gets wet from perspiration, stop the game and wipe up the moisture before someone slips. Be aware of where other players are before you swing your racquet, and stay out of the way when someone else is swinging one. A swat with a racquet isn't usually dangerous, but it can put you out of the game for a while.

## The Court

You don't really need a court to start playing racquetball. Many good handball players got their training by using a basement wall or the side of a building, and you can do the same with racquetball. Just be sure you find a place that's away from traffic. Stay away from windows, and also from anyone who might be annoyed by the constant thumping of the ball.

Racquetball can be played in a handball court that has only one or three walls, but competitive racquetball is played in a four wall court with a ceiling. The court is 20 feet wide, 40 feet long, and 20 feet high. In this book, we'll be using such a court in order to describe all of the possible shots. You'll have six playing surfaces—the front wall, back wall, two side walls, the ceiling, and the floor. Playing in such an enclosed area encourages beginners because they don't have to cover a huge expanse of space.

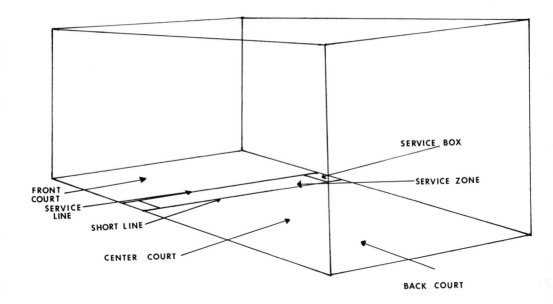

SERVICE BOX

SERVICE ZONE

FRONT
COURT
SERVICE
LINE

SHORT LINE

CENTER COURT

BACK COURT

Lines divide the court into different sections. The *short line* runs parallel to the front wall. It divides the court into two equal sections: the *front court* and the *back court*. The *service line* is five feet in front of the short line, and parallel to it. The area between the short line and the service line is the *service zone*.

At either end of the service zone, 18 inches from the side wall, are two lines that run parallel to the side walls. These lines form the *service boxes*. In a game of doubles, the server's partner must stand in one of these boxes during the serve.

If you're playing against an ordinary wall, you can use chalk or tape to divide the playing area into the proper sections.

You and your friends may be among the smaller beginning players. If so, you may want to start off with a half court to make up for your shorter arms and legs. You can do this in two ways—either by marking the regular court in half from side wall to side wall, or from front wall to back wall. In the side wall to side wall way, you can use tape to mark the playing areas within that smaller space. Of course, as your game improves, you'll want to graduate to full court.

It's a good idea to watch experienced players in action as often as you can. The excitement of the game is catching, and you may decide to start practicing harder. Who knows, maybe someday you'll be a pro yourself!

Another thing to learn from watching good players is that even they sometimes misjudge their shots. Knowing this, you'll not be nearly so discouraged when you goof.

# ③

# *The Game*

The main object in a game of racquetball is to prevent your opponent from returning the ball to you. To accomplish this purpose, you must hit the ball to where he isn't. Make him run, force him to ''dig'' the ball out of a corner, hit the ball high over his head.

To start the game, the server stands inside the service zone. He drops the ball to the floor at least once, but not more than three times, then hits it with his racquet. The ball must rebound off the front wall, then touch the floor in back of the short line *before* the server can leave the service box. If he steps out, he has committed a *fault*. If he commits two faults in a row, he loses the serve.

Here are some other serving faults.

1. A *short serve*, in which the ball bounces off the front wall and rebounds in front of the short line.
2. A *long serve*, in which the ball touches the back wall without touching the floor first.
3. A *ceiling ball,* in which a served ball strikes the ceiling.
4. A *three wall serve,* in which the ball rebounds from the front wall to one side wall and then to the other side wall without touching the floor in between them.

When the served ball doesn't touch the front wall before touching another playing surface, it's a *non-front serve* and an *out*. An out means a loss of the serve.

An out also occurs when:

1. The served ball bounces off the front wall and hits the server.
2. The ball is missed during an attempted serve.
3. The ball hits any part of the server's body during the serve attempt.

After the serve, the receiver must return the ball before it touches the floor twice. His return shot has to touch the front wall before it hits the floor. The play then continues until either the server or the receiver is unable to return the ball.

A *rally* is the exchange of shots between serves. Only the server can win any points during the rally. If the server fails to return the ball, the receiver becomes the server. He then serves, and another rally begins. The game ends when one player gets 21 points.

A *match* consists of three games. If each player has won

a game, an 11 or 15 point tie breaker may be played to determine the winner of the match.

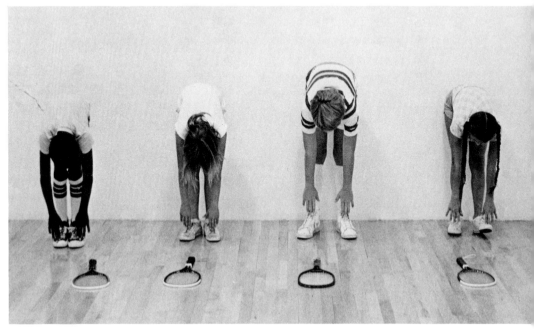

*Some warm-up exercises: bending, stretching, twisting.*

Now it's time to start learning the grips and strokes of racquetball. But before each practice session, you should spend at least five minutes in warm-up exercises. Jogging in place, jumping rope, knee bends, and stretching exercises are all recommended. Professional football and baseball players always warm up before they play. You should, too, unless you *want* to have pulled muscles and ligaments.

In both your warm ups and your actual playing, concentrate on moving smoothly and naturally. Flowing motions will

give you better results than brute strength. Controlled movements give you better shots than wild, jerky swings. You should feel relaxed and "springy," not tense and nervous. This type of playing will prevent sore muscles and pulled tendons.

# Basic Grips and Strokes

## The Forehand Grip

The first important thing to learn in racquetball is how to hold the racquet. Why is this step necessary? After all, anyone can see where the handle is. All you have to do is pick it up. Right?

Wrong! This step is so important that many instructors spend a whole lesson just teaching the correct grip. They know that a small mistake in the grip makes a big difference in where the ball goes.

The basic forehand grip consists first of "shaking hands"

*The forehand grip.*

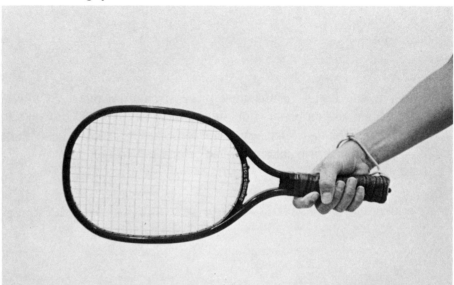

with the handle. Your thumb and your forefinger should form a V. To get that V in the right position, turn the racquet until it's even or parallel with the wall. Now curl your last three fingers firmly, yet comfortably, around the handle. Bend your index finger as if you were pulling a trigger, then extend it beyond your thumb.

Your entire palm should be on the handle. Don't let the end of the handle slide out. If you do, you'll lose some of your control over the racquet.

To test your grip, hold the racquet straight out in front of you. You shouldn't be able to see the strings at all. Swing it around. Does it wobble, or feel insecure in your hand? If it does, double check your hand and finger position. You should feel as if you're in complete control of the racquet's movement.

If you have small hands, you may not be able to keep the racquet from wobbling even with the correct grip. In that case, slide your playing hand up on the handle an inch or two and grasp

*The two-handed grip.*

the end of the handle with your other hand. Many young players have competed successfully using this two-handed grip.

## The Ready Position

The ready position is the way you stand and hold the racquet while you're waiting for your opponent to hit the ball.

Both of your feet should be on the ground, and no further apart than the width of your shoulders. Bend your knees slightly, but don't stiffen them. Lean forward just a little from your waist. Hold your racquet waist high and straight out in front of you.

In the instructions which follow, it is assumed that you are right handed. If you're a leftie, change the word *right* to *left* and the word *left* to *right*.

*The ready position.*

# Forehand Stroke

This is the easiest and most natural stroke in racquetball. For this reason, it's easy to think that you don't need much practice to perfect it. However, every fifteen minutes you spend getting your forehand in shape will pay big dividends on the court. It's the single most important stroke in the game. You can play about two-thirds of all of the court positions using your forehand, and it's an important part of almost all your basic shots.

**1.** Stand in the ready position. As the ball approaches on your right, turn in that direction by pivoting on the balls of your feet. Keep your knees slightly bent.

2. Bend your right elbow, and bring your arm as far back of your right shoulder as you can. The racquet head should be pointing toward the ceiling. Put your weight onto your right foot and *cock*, or stiffen, your wrist.

3. As you start to swing the racquet toward the ball, shift your weight onto your left foot. Keep your back straight, and begin to straighten your arm.

4. The *contact point,* the point at which the racquet and the ball meet, should be at knee level and even with your left foot. At this instant your arm should be straight. *Uncock*, or *snap* your wrist as you hit the ball.

5. After contact point, let your arm continue its natural swing across your body. This follow-through is essential to the smoothness and power of your stroke. It will

also help you keep your balance. When the racquet stops, it should be even with your left shoulder. Return immediately to the ready position.

In the forehand, as with all strokes, your left, or non-playing arm, should be used to balance your body weight. The only time it will be near or touching the racquet is during the ready position. When you start your stroke, it should be moving *away* from your body.

As you start to practice the forehand stroke, your contact point can be about waist high. Gradually, get it down to knee level, and even lower. All skilled players hit the ball as close to the floor as possible.

Volley off the wall until your forehand feels smooth, and all of the movements flow together in one continuous motion. After you get the feel of that flowing motion, work on hitting the ball as hard as you can. If you're doing the stroke correctly, the power should come without too much conscious effort on your part.

Try to imagine the swing actually starts in your feet, travels upward through your legs, into your body and your shoulders, and down through your arms. When you hit the ball, that snap of your wrist should release all of the energy you've built up. Your follow-through should be a natural continuation of the release of that power.

When you have the feel and the power of the stroke, work on accuracy. Mark several places on the wall with tape and aim the ball at them. Keep practicing until you can hit your target every time. Then move around the court and hit it from different positions.

If you find that you're having trouble with aiming the ball, check the following points.

1. Is your arm fully extended at contact point? Don't "crowd" the ball.
2. Are you shifting your weight to the proper foot at the proper time?
3. Watch the angle of your racquet at contact point. If it's tilted upward, the ball will go up. If it's tilted downward, the ball will go down. If it's even, or not tilted, the ball will go to the wall in a straight line.

To keep the racquet from tilting, check your grip. Also, try to keep your shoulders from dipping during your swing. Your back should be straight, and your shoulders on a line with each other.

## The Backhand

The backhand stroke runs a close second in importance to the forehand. Considering this fact, it's amazing that only a few of the more advanced racquetball players have a strong, reliable backhand. If you develop this stroke, you'll be a giant step ahead of your competitors.

*A backhand shot.*

5553

The backhand motion isn't nearly as natural a motion as the forehand. On the other hand, with practice it can be made to feel natural. It can be made into an even more powerful stroke than the forehand because the entire motion is completely away from your body.

## Backhand Grip

The backhand grip involves just one small change from the forehand grip. It will make a big difference in the power and accuracy of your stroke.

Hold your racquet with the basic forehand grip. Then slide the V about half an inch to the left, or toward yourself.

Simple? Yes, but don't let that fool you. This grip will help make your backhand a winner.

## Backhand Stroke

1. Stand in the ready position. As the ball approaches on your left, pivot toward it on the balls of your feet.

2. Put your weight on your left foot. Bend your right arm, and bring the racquet across your body until it's above your left shoulder and pointing toward the ceiling. Rotate your shoulders in the same direction. Cock your wrist toward your body.

3. As you continue your backswing, shift your weight onto your right foot. Follow the swing with your shoulders and straighten your arm. Contact point should be near your right knee with your arm fully extended. Uncock your wrist as you hit the ball.

**4.** Follow-through should continue until your arm stops naturally in back of your right side.

Start the practice of your backhand by hitting the ball at waist level, then gradually lower the contact point. Don't crowd the ball, and keep your shoulders level as you rotate them.

Concentrate on the smoothness and power of this stroke before you become concerned about the accuracy. Slam the ball as hard as you can, while controlling the motion of your body. Power plus control will lead to winning shots.

# The Overhead Drive

The ball is approaching high and is losing speed. If you don't return it right away, you'll lose the point. If you're an average player, you'll panic, bend backward, become unbalanced, and take a desperate last minute swipe at the ball. If you succeed in hitting it at all, there'll be no power or direction to the stroke.

But you're a better than average player, and you're going to catch your opponent off guard with a smashing overhead drive. You might even be able to "kill" the ball, so he won't be able to return it at all.

The motion in the overhead drive is the same one you'd use in throwing a ball.

**1.** Use the forehand grip, and stand in the ready position. Face sideways in relation to the path of the ball.

2. As the ball approaches, bring the racquet down close to the right side of your body, past your right foot, and as far back as you can. Your arm should be straight.

3. Bend your elbow and twist your arm to bring the racquet back and up until it's level with your head. Straighten your arm and continue to raise the racquet. Shift your weight forward onto your left foot. Cock your wrist.

4. Contact point should occur above your head and about a foot in front of your right shoulder. Uncock your wrist.

5. Let your body flow forward naturally during the follow-through. Your arm should come down across your body until the racquet has passed your left knee. (The photo below shows the awkward position in which the player could be left.)

If this stroke isn't done properly, it could result in sore muscles or tennis elbow. The trick is to hit the ball over your shoulder with a straight arm. It isn't necessary to use a lot of force with the overhead drive. Most of the power will come from the proper use of your body, and the uncocking of your wrist. Too much force may throw you off balance during the follow-through.

Being thrown off balance is one of the risks in this stroke. It also leaves you in a bad playing position with your arm stretched awkwardly across your body. Nevertheless, at the right time it can be a very useful shot.

You can practice these basic strokes by yourself using any wall that's handy. First of all, travel the length of the wall while doing twenty forehands. Next, come back along the wall doing twenty backhands. Now, stand in one place and do twenty overhead drives.

It's also helpful to get a friend involved in your practice sessions. Ask him to hit to both your forehand and backhand sides with an occasional high shot to make you use your overhead. Keep an eye on the ball as it approaches. Try to have the ball strike the center of your racquet. That's where you'll be able to get your most powerful and accurate strokes.

Start forming good habits right from the start. Getting into ready position, your backswing, your follow-through—all of these things should eventually become completely automatic. When that happens, you'll be able to concentrate on putting the ball exactly where you want it.

Accuracy is extremely important in racquetball. Many beginners think that by simply hitting the ball as hard as they can, they can win games. If you work on placing your shots in the right places, *you'll* be the one who's winning.

# (5)

# *Serves*

In racquetball, as in tennis, the serve is where the action begins. As the server, you have a big opportunity to determine just what direction that action will take. First, the serve is the only shot that lets you take your time. You can look around, observe your opponent, set up, or get into position, and execute a good strong stroke. You have plenty of room, and no pressure forcing you to make a split second decision.

Secondly, of course, you're the only one who can earn any points during the rally, or the exchange of shots that follows

**The server and the receiver.**

the serve. Third, you start the rally in center court position, which means that you're able to move quickly and directly to any other part of the court. Fourth, a good strong serve to your opponent's backhand will almost always mean that he'll make a weak, defensive return. You'll be in control of the rally right from the start.

In its simplest form, the serve merely starts the rally. You can see how a smart player will turn it into much more than that.

## The Power Drive

Of the two basic serves, the power drive is the most important and the most commonly used by skilled players. If you can master it, you're well on the way to controlling rallies.

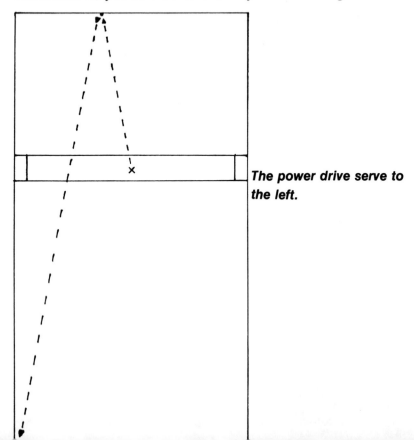

**The power drive serve to the left.**

This shot should be hit hard, and aimed between the center and the corner of the front wall. It will then travel toward the back wall low and fast. It should *die*, or roll to a stop, after hitting the back side wall near the corner.

Use a long, free, graceful stroke. Keep your racquet head even, and hit the ball in a straight line to the front wall.

1. Stand in the center of the service zone and face the right wall. Place your feet several inches apart with your left foot about 12 inches ahead of your right foot. Bend your knees slightly.
2. Hold the ball in your left hand and straight out in front of your chest. Drop it—don't throw it—to the floor. As it bounces upward, straighten your right arm and bring the racquet as far back of your right shoulder as you can. At the same time, put your weight onto your right foot and cock your wrist.

**The correct serving position.**

3. Swing the racquet forward, and shift your weight onto your left foot. Lean toward the ball, but don't crowd it. At contact point, your arm should still be straight and the ball about knee level. Uncock your wrist.
4. The follow-through should pull your body forward and around, so you'll end up facing the front wall ready to return the receiver's shot. Look over your shoulder to watch your opponent. His motions may give you an idea of how he plans to return the serve.

At this point, it's a good idea to mention that in racquetball *you should avoid turning your back to the front wall*. One reason for this rule is that you'll be in a better position to play when you're facing forward. Another important reason is that you'll lessen your chances of getting hit in the back by an unseen ball. Remember that *all* shots are going to be played off the front wall. You'll want to be ready for them.

## Lob Serve

The lob serve is a high-altitude, low-speed shot. Many top players use it for a variety of reasons. First, there are times when a power drive just doesn't do the job it's supposed to do. Maybe you're tired, or your opponent is returning your best fast shots much too easily. Second, slowing the pace of the game will give you more time to prepare for the return. If you can control the pace, you'll be better able to control the rally.

Third, if your opponent is expecting another power drive, the lob serve will catch him off guard. The more you can keep him guessing, the better off you'll be.

The lob serve should be aimed at the front wall at least eight feet above the floor, and about halfway between where

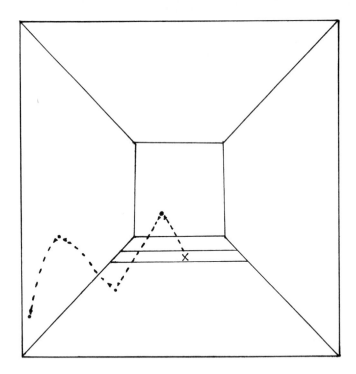

you're standing and the left side wall. The ball should come off the front wall, bounce on the floor three or four feet past the short line, rise in a high arc, and hit the side wall about seven or eight feet from a back corner. It will then bounce softly and roll to a stop. Besides having to run for it, the receiver will have to play it close to the side wall, which is not easy.

1. Stand in the center of the service zone and face the front wall. Your left foot should be in front, and your right foot about 12 inches behind it. Bend your knees slightly.

2. Hold the ball at arm's length in front of your chest and drop it. At the same time, bring your racquet down and past your right leg. With your elbow slightly bent, bring your arm back as far as you can. At this point, your weight should be on both feet.

3. Swing your arm down and forward, and face the ball. Let your racquet come up underneath it.
4. At contact point, which is at waist or chest level and above your right foot, your arm should be straight and your body toward the ball. Shift your weight onto your left foot. *Don't* uncock your wrist, or the ball will travel too fast.
5. Follow through by bringing your racquet forward and up until it stops naturally above the left side of your head.

Whenever possible, hit this, and any other shot, to your opponent's backhand side. If he's an average player, his backhand will be weak.

Judge the lob's speed and direction carefully. If the ball doesn't hit the side wall, you'll be handing the receiver an easy return. If it's going too fast, it will hit the side wall, then bounce off the back wall, giving your opponent a "plum," or a good set up.

It's almost as bad to hit the side wall too far forward. In that case, the ball will rebound into center court. Result? Another plum for the receiver.

## The Z Serve

Many players don't consider the Z shot a basic serve, but it's a good one to know so that you can keep your opponent confused. As you can probably guess, this shot takes its name from the twisty path it follows.

In an ideal Z serve, the ball will strike the front wall 8 to 16 feet above the floor. It will then rebound forcefully onto the side wall and travel across the court. After bouncing on the floor,

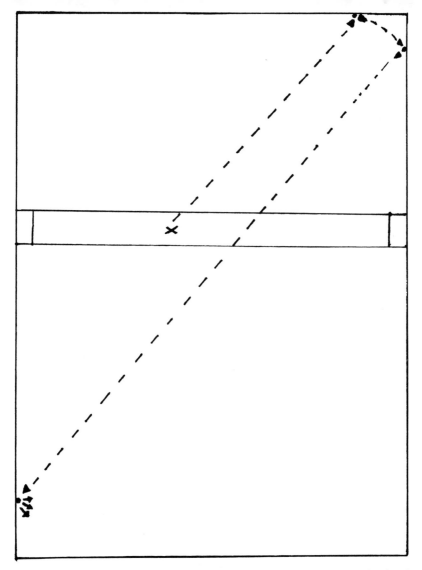

it will hit the opposite side wall about 2 or 3 inches from the back wall. The ball should not hit the first side wall before hitting the front wall. That's a fault. And the ball must bounce on the floor before it hits the back side wall. Otherwise, it's a three-wall serve—another fault.

There's a good chance the ball will hit you as it crosses the court. Not only will that hurt, but you'll lose the serve. Stay out of its way.

Stand on one side of the service zone and face the right side wall. Use the same stroke that you use for a power drive. Aiming about two or three feet from the corner and high up on the front wall, hit the ball *sharply*. Uncock your wrist at contact point. Move out of the ball's path.

In the 1972 International Singles Championship match between Charlie Brumfield and Ron Rubenstein, Brumfield used the Z ball to make Rubenstein shoot weak returns.

"He drove me crazy with those Z balls," Rubenstein said. "There was absolutely nothing I could do with them. The Z ball got me off balance and in deep (back) court, and all I could do was flick the ball off the front wall."

There you are—a way to drive your opponent crazy. If he can't return your serve, you'll have an "ace," which adds a point to your score.

During your practice sessions, learn your serves the same way you learned your basic shots. First, practice the correct arm and foot movements for the serves. See how well you can control the ball's speed.

Don't forget the importance of accuracy. Place a towel on the floor and see if you can make the ball rebound off the wall and land in the center of the towel. Practice one shot again and again until you can hit the towel every time. If you can do this, you'll start to feel confident about your ability to make the ball do what you want it to do. Carry this confidence and know-how into your next game.

One last suggestion—keep a sharp eye on your opponent after you serve the ball. If you've hit the shot correctly, you already know where the ball is going to go. You also know that he must return it to the front wall. Face the front wall, get into ready position, and look over your shoulder. Watch your opponent's leg and arm movements so you'll know what's on his mind.

Always assume that your shot will be returned, no matter how terrific your serve was. If you're not ready for the ball, it may bounce on the floor twice before you're able to return it. And *that* means you've lost the serve.

As you practice these serves and the other shots in this book, don't worry if the ball doesn't go where you want it to go right away. Keep trying, and enjoy your practice sessions. Just batting the ball around will help you become more familiar with the various strokes and what paths the ball will take.

And if the shot *does* work for you, can you do it again? And again and again?

# ⑥

# *Serve Returns*

Your job as the receiver of a serve is to give the server as hard a time as possible. What you want, after all, is to trade places with him. As a receiver, you're on the defensive. You're in back court instead of center court. And you have no chance to score. To avoid spending too much time in this undesirable position, you should use as many hours practicing your serve returns as you do the serves themselves.

The normal serve return position is two to four feet from the back wall, and halfway between the side walls. Face the server in the ready position. Be prepared to run in any direction, although most servers will aim to your left, or your backhand.

Watch your opponent carefully, and try to decide from his motions what he is planning to do. After he has hit the ball, decide instantly how you're going to return it. In racquetball, even a wrong reaction is better than no reaction at all. The idea is to think fast and get moving.

If the ball is approaching on your left, pivot on your left foot, and take your first step with your right foot. Do the opposite if the ball is approaching on your right. You should get within striking range with as few motions as possible. Make every movement and every second count.

Don't crowd the ball. Leave plenty of room for a full,

*A bird's-eye view of server and receiver.*

free stroke. Whenever it's possible, save your energy and let the ball come to you. A good general rule is: if the ball is below knee level, run toward it and return it. If it's above knee level, wait for it to rebound off a wall. By doing so, you'll have more time to set up.

Here are some of the official rules for serve returns.

1. While the ball is being served, you must stand at least five feet in back of the short line.
2. You must not return the ball until it has passed the short line.

3. You may return the ball before it touches the floor, or "on the fly." You *must* return it before it touches the floor twice.
4. Your return must send the ball to the front wall, but it can hit the ceiling or one or both side walls first. It must *not* touch the floor before it touches the front wall.
5. When you swing at a serve and miss, you don't automatically lose the rally. If you recover quickly enough to make a legal return, you're still in the running.

There are two commonly used types of serve returns—pass shots, which are offensive, and ceiling shots which are defensive.

# Pass Shots

### Down-the-Wall Pass

This shot should hit the front wall, travel close to the side wall into the back court, and die before hitting the back wall. Its purpose is to make the server leave the center court and play the ball close to the wall.

Aim the ball close to the corner of the front wall. Hit it hard enough to fly past your opponent on the rebound, but not hard enough to bounce off the back wall.

### Cross-Court Pass

This shot should strike the front wall, cross the court, then rebound off the side wall in the back court. Aim the ball at the front wall just off center. Use enough force to drive it past center court on the rebound.

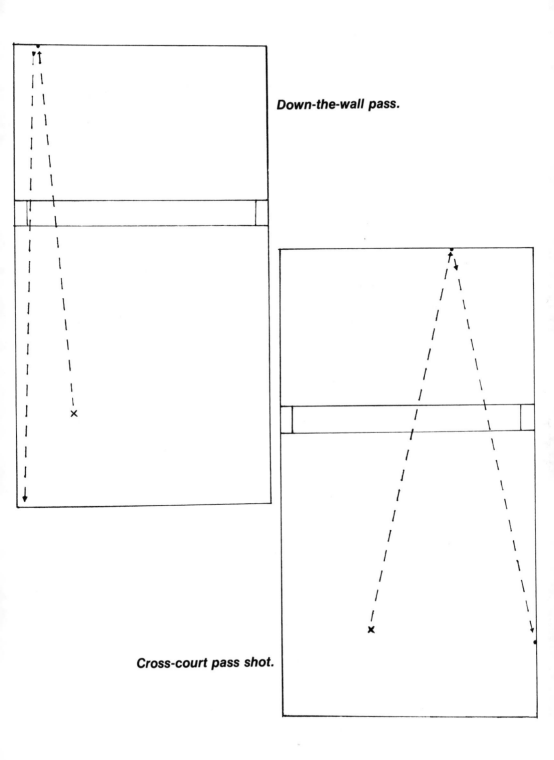

*Down-the-wall pass.*

*Cross-court pass shot.*

# Ceiling Return

Offensive shots are generally used when you're feeling aggressive and confident. Use a ceiling return when you're tired and want to "buy" some time to catch your breath and set up for your next shot. Your opponent will be forced to run into back court, and you'll be better able to advance to center court. The more you can make him run, and the more time you spend in center court, the better you'll be able to control the rally.

Use the overhand stroke and tilt the racquet face upward. Contact point should be above head level. Uncock your wrist. The ball should strike the ceiling two to five feet in front of the front wall. It should then drop down to the front wall, rebound to the floor near the short line, and bounce high. Ideally, it will die near a back corner.

The best ceiling shot is a *wallpaper ball,* which clings to the side wall as it drops into back court.

**Return ceiling ball.**

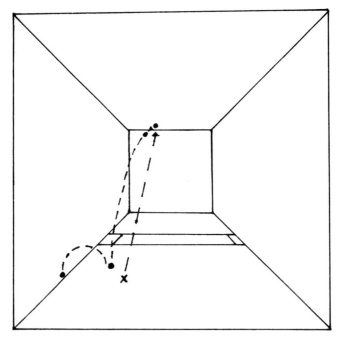

Learn to judge the speed of this shot. If you hit it too softly, it will give the server time to react and hit it back easily. If you give the shot too much power, it may rebound off the back wall instead of dying. Result? Your opponent has a second chance at it.

Also, watch where you aim your ceiling shots. They must hit the ceiling close to the front wall. If they hit further back, they will rebound into center court, giving your opponent a perfect set up.

## Some Hints for Receivers

1. Use pass shots to make your opponent run to the front or the side walls. Use ceiling shots to make him run into back court.
2. Be as confident and aggressive a receiver as you can be. If you can "fake out" your opponent by always being ready to pounce on his serve, and by taking advantage of his mistakes, he'll be much more likely to start serving more bad serves than good.
3. Don't allow your returns to bounce off the back wall.
4. Use different types of shots to confuse your opponent. Vary your patterns of play.
5. If you return the serve on the fly, be careful not to step into the service zone. If you do, your return will be illegal.
6. After your return, immediately move toward center court, and get into the ready position. Keep one eye on the ball, and the other on your opponent. As the ball comes back to you, get your racquet into striking position and cock your wrist.

**7.** *Don't forget the basics.* Quick reactions and good decisions don't mean anything if you just chop and flick at the ball. Use your legs, shoulders, and the correct motions of your playing arm and wrist to smash the ball back.

Learn to "turn the tables" on the server. If he serves a power drive, use it to your advantage. If it's approaching high, wait until it comes off the back wall and slam it back to him. If it's approaching low, hit it back right away. The ball's speed, plus your quick reaction, will give your opponent less time to set up.

To return a lob serve which is high and losing speed fast, hit the ball before it bounces near the short line, or immediately afterward. Don't let it bounce over your head and out of reach. If the ball is high and *not* losing speed, let it rebound off the back wall. You'll have a perfect set up and a terrific return.

To return the Z serve, hit the ball either right before or right after it bounces off the side wall. Don't wait to see if it's going to rebound off the back wall. There's a good chance it will die before it does. As Charlie Brumfield says, "Once the ball is in the hitting area, you'd better be ready to strike it without hesitating. Otherwise, the ball will get past you, and then you're not going to be able to hit it anywhere."

Practice these returns and their variations by standing in the back court and hitting the wall with varying degrees of force. Aim it at target areas on the front wall or ceiling. Use both your backhand and your forehand. Work regularly on your overhand.

Get up a serve-return game with a friend. For every serve that isn't returned, the server gets a point. For every return the server misses, the receiver gets a point. The first side to get 21 points wins.

Another good two-player drill is the cross-court drill. One player will stand in the back corner and hit a down-the-wall pass; the second player will return it with a cross-court pass. Do this drill ten times, then switch places. You'll learn your pass shots, *and* learn to run.

# *The Rally*

If the serve is where the action *begins,* the rally is where the action *is.* It's here that your planning, training, and endurance will be tested.

Every racquetball shot must be played off the front wall, including, of course, the initial serve and the serve return. During the rally, either player may hit the ball so that it touches *any* playing surface, or combination of playing surfaces, before and after it touches the front wall. The only restriction is that the ball must not touch the floor before hitting the front wall.

During a rally, you can use one or both hands to make a shot. However, you cannot switch from one hand to the other to strike the ball. That's an out or a point for your opponent.

*The player who controls center court controls the rally.* From center court, any shot can be hit successfully, and you're only a few feet away from returning any shot. Also, it doesn't take nearly as much power or accuracy to hit a ball to the front wall from that position as it does to hit it from the back court.

At the beginning of the rally, the server has this choice spot. It's the receiver's job to force him out of center court by the way he places his shots. As the server runs to the side wall or to a back corner to return the ball, the receiver should immediately advance to center court, and prepare to defend his position. Now it's the server's task to move the receiver into back court.

Move to center court. Force your opponent out of center court. That's what the rally is all about. And the only way to accomplish this goal is by planning and skill, because one of the basic rules of racquetball is that the players stay out of each other's way. You *must* give your opponent a clear, straight path to the front wall. You can't obstruct his swing in any way. You must stay out of the path of his ball. If you don't follow these rules, you'll find that you have committed a *hinder,* or an obstruction.

There are avoidable hinders, which occur when someone is careless or gets in someone's way on purpose. These result in the loss of the serve, or in a point for the server, depending upon who committed the hinder.

There are also unavoidable hinders, which are purely accidental and which could not have been easily prevented. In these cases, the point is played over.

Whether or not a hinder could have been easily prevented may cause some arguments. It's better not to be too stubborn whenever there's a disagreement. Just back down gracefully, and maybe the next time it happens your opponent will be more inclined to see things your way.

Most hinders are avoidable if the players use common

sense and keep their wits about them. Occasionally, someone is going to get hit by a ball because he or his opponent didn't think or react fast enough. Once in a while, someone may get hit by a swinging racquet. In this case, both players may be responsible. The one who was struck may have been crowding his opponent. On the other hand, the one who did the striking may not have been watching what he was doing.

It's easy to become fearful when you've been hit by a ball or a racquet once or twice. Some players react by staying close to the walls and avoiding center court. That's a bad habit to get into. It won't do your game or your self-esteem any good. Most injuries are suffered by beginning players who haven't learned to stay clear of flying and swinging objects. Safety is just a matter of keeping your eyes open and your mind alert.

During a rally, you're going to need a variety of shots to keep your opponent running to the back and side walls. Don't let your game fall into a predictable pattern. You don't want anyone except you to know what you're going to do next.

## V Pass

The V pass is commonly used by good players when their opponent is in center or front court. It's a simple cross-court type of shot that travels in a wide V path. Hit it as low as you can, and with more force than you would use in a down the wall pass.

If you're on the right side of the court, aim just to the left of the center of the front wall. If you're on the left side, aim to the right of center. On the rebound, the ball should hit the side wall near the short line, then head for the opposite back corner.

Don't let your ball rebound in front of the short line. If

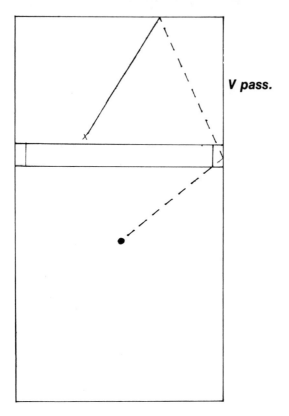

**V pass.**

you do, your opponent will have an easy shot from center court. But don't let it hit so far back that it rebounds off the back wall.

This pass can be made from nearly every court position and from almost any height. However, the ball will take a different angle when you hit it from different locations. When you practice, try to have someone hit the ball to you, so you'll have to run for it. Hit it both high and low as you move around the court. Remember what angles the ball takes and how it rebounds, and notice the spot on the front wall where you hit the ball to get these flight paths.

The V pass can also be used as a serve. Simply aim close enough to the side wall so it will be sure to fly past the short line, and hit it medium hard.

# The High Lob

Both the high lob and the medium lob (see lob serve) can be used effectively in the rally, if they are used at the right times. Charlie Brumfield uses the lob as a change-of-pace shot.

"Most advanced racquetball is played at a slam-bang rate of speed," he says. "If in a hard, fast, tense game you can manage to hit a high soft lob at your opponent, he may be so surprised that he will rush his shot and hit an ineffective return. Hitting a slow lob gives me more time to get in a good position to cover my opponent's return."

Hit the lob softly, but firmly. A high lob should touch the front wall about 15 or 16 feet above the floor. It should then touch the side wall as it descends into back court, but should *not* rebound off the back wall. If it does, you're hitting it too hard. Concentrate on a light, firm stroke instead of a long, powerful swing.

# Ceiling Shots

A well placed ceiling shot can also break up the fast pace of the game. Steve Keeley is an expert ceiling ball player. He uses this shot often to change the pattern of a tough rally.

"The player should always try to hit the ceiling ball two to five feet back from the front wall," he advises. "If your ball strays too far from the front wall, you'll have to hit it much harder to make it bounce into back court."

Use these shots, not only for the initial serve return, but in other situations when your opponent isn't expecting them. You can use your backhand for a ceiling ball, if contact point is shoulder high instead of over your head. When you begin your backhand stroke, your right foot should be in front and your weight on your left foot. When the ball is about a foot away, bring the racquet toward it, and shift your weight onto your right foot. Tilt the racquet face to drive the ball to the correct spot on the ceiling. Uncock your wrist and follow through naturally.

You can also hit a ceiling shot with a contact point as low as knee level. Drop your right shoulder as you start your swing, and step toward the ball with your right foot. The dropping of your shoulder plus the correct upward tilt of your racquet and the sharp uncocking of your wrist at contact point will result in an effective ceiling ball. It will also result in a surprise for your opponent.

## Kill Shots

A kill shot is like a batter hitting the ball to the fences in a baseball game, or a football player taking a chance on a long pass. There's a risk involved in both of these situations, but sometimes it's worth the gamble.

In racquetball, if your kill shot goes wrong, you'll probably lose the serve, or give your opponent a point. But if things go right, you've saved yourself a lot of running and effort, and you've probably unnerved your opponent. No matter how skilled a player you are, you're never going to be a consistent winner unless you know how and when to kill the ball.

To be effective, the kill shot must be hit so low that it bounces twice before your opponent can get to it. A *rollout* is a perfect kill shot. It's hit so hard that it hits the front wall, then simply rolls onto the floor. Such an unreturnable shot can be either a dream or a nightmare, depending on whether you're on the sending or receiving end of it.

**Contact point for a kill shot.**

All champions use kills whenever they see a chance for one. Charlie Brumfield estimates that he tries one kill return out of every ten shots, "just to keep'em guessing."

And the really smart players also know when *not* to try a kill. Many beginners have given up on this type of shot because they kept using them at the wrong times and failing.

Before you even consider a kill, you must be in a good stroking position. Such a shot depends on both power and accuracy.

"It is very important to hit kill shots at below knee level," says Bill Schmidtke, who won the 1971 International Singles Championship. "I really get down there. I bend my back and my knees, reach out about a foot from my body, and hit the ball slightly more than a racquet's width above the floor. Sometimes I get so low that I actually scrape my hand on the floor."

The ideal kill situation is where you have plenty of time to set up and plenty of room for your stroke. It's even better when you're in center court, and your opponent is in back court. And watch for the times when your opponent makes a mistake, such as letting a ball rebound off the back or side wall into your range. You should almost always go for a kill shot when you have such a chance.

**Straight Kill**

In this kill, you should be standing near the side wall so you can hit the ball straight and hard into the front wall very near the corner. If your contact point is below knee level, the ball should die shortly after striking the front wall.

Experienced players use the straight kill in about 70% of all their kill attempts. They like it because it strikes only one surface, so there is less chance of anything going wrong.

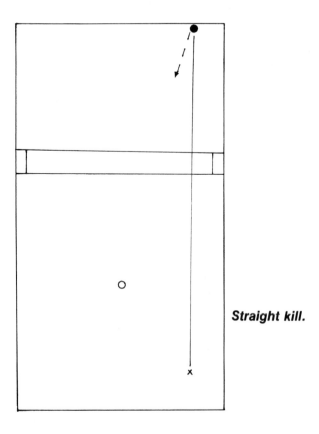

*Straight kill.*

## Corner Kills

Corner kills are effective when they are hit to the front corner opposite your opponent. They don't have to be hit quite as low or quite as hard as the straight kill, because the two-wall combination will help to slow the ball.

## Side Wall to Front Wall (Pinch Shot)

Aim fairly low at either side wall. The ball should hit the side wall about three feet away from the front wall. It should rebound onto the front wall, then bounce off and die. This shot can be hit from any court position, but it's best used when your opponent is somewhere behind you, or to one side of you.

"I use the side wall kill if my opponent is behind me," says Bill Schmidtke. "By the time he reacts to the shot hitting the side wall, it's too late for him to retrieve the ball at the front wall."

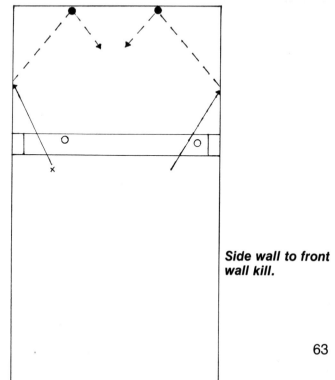

*Side wall to front wall kill.*

## Front Wall to Side Wall

This kill shot is risky, because the ball rebounds off the side wall right into center court if it doesn't die soon enough. As a result, you should use it *only* when your opponent is in back court. To lessen the chances of the shot going wrong, hit the ball to the same side of the court that you are on. If you're on the right side, aim at the right side of the front wall at a point no higher than thigh level. The ball should rebound to the side wall near the floor.

Bill Schmidtke attempts this shot only when his opponent is out of position in back court. "Otherwise the chances for a set up off a missed shot are just too great," he says.

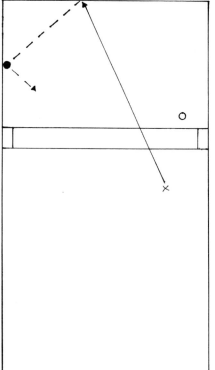

**Front wall to side wall kill.**

## The Drop Shot

The drop shot is also a form of kill which is good to use when you're in center court and your opponent is in back court. Aim the ball low at the front wall near the corner. Strike it firmly, but with a shortened stroke. *Don't* uncock your wrist, and *don't* use any follow-through. The motion is more of a pushing one than a hitting one, somewhat like a bunt in baseball.

There should be very little rebound if this shot is done properly. The ball will die before your opponent can run up to get it.

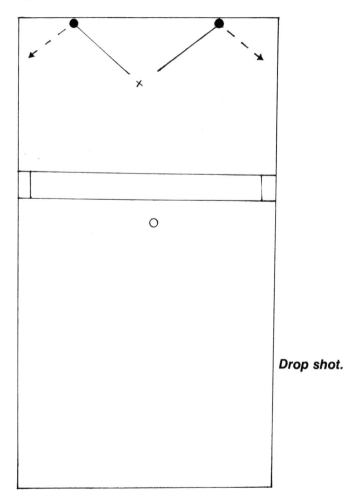

**Drop shot.**

Practice these kills until you can do them automatically at the right time. And don't forget that you have a backhand as well as a forehand. Ron Rubenstein says, "I can't stress enough the importance of practice. The player should get out on the court and hit backhand kills over and over again. I get so I could hit kills in my sleep."

You should practice so many kills that the motions are "programmed" into you. Keep your contact point low, and don't tilt the racquet head. If it's tilted up, the ball will go too high on the wall. If it's tilted down, the ball may skip onto the floor and stop before reaching the front wall.

## Overhead Shots

As you've been told, the overhead is a risky shot, but it can be used instead of the ceiling shot to change the pace of the rally. Don't forget to practice it so you can pull it out of your bag of tricks to stun your opponent.

## The Overhead Drive

Use this shot when you've been forced into back court by a high-bouncing ball, and you don't feel like slowing down the rally with a ceiling ball.

Aim straight for the front wall at a point about three or four feet above the floor. Don't hit it too hard, or it may end up rebounding off the back wall.

# The Overhead Kill

This is a tough shot, but it's worth perfecting. Since you use the same motions for this kill as you do for a ceiling ball, your opponent won't be prepared for what happens. Use it when both of you are in back court. It's unlikely that he'll get to the front wall in time to return it.

Use the overhead stroke and make your contact point around head level. Tilt your racquet downward so that the ball angles into the front wall as low and as close to the corner as possible.

As you practice these shots, keep changing your court position and observe the angles the ball takes as it rebounds off the wall. Does it rebound onto a side wall from the front wall? Does it roll onto the floor? Does it bounce far into the court, or does it cling to the side wall? When you are able to get just the results you want, practice that same shot in the same way again and again. Program it into your head so that you will have it when you're in an exciting competition.

# (8)

# Back Wall, Back Corner, and Side Wall Play

You've practiced your basic strokes until you can do them automatically. You've learned how to return a lob serve, and how to kill a ball. You know that you're going to have to control center court in order to win.

Are you now ready to challenge the champs?

Not quite. What are you going to do when the ball clings to the side wall, or when it angles crazily out of a back corner? Do you know how to take full advantage of a ball that rebounds from the back wall? You won't be a real expert until you can *read* the ball, or predict the path it will take as it bounces off walls and corners.

## Back Wall Play

When your opponent's shot goes wrong, and the ball rebounds off the back wall while you're in back court, you've received a gift. The problem is that unless you know how to use that gift, it won't do you any good.

Many otherwise good players haven't brushed up on their back wall play because they've forgotten an important fact—racquetball is *not* just another form of tennis. In tennis, once the ball has sailed past you, you might as well forget it. Not so in racquetball. In fact, there are times when you've made a mistake by not letting it go on to the back wall. Remember that basic rule—the one that goes: if the ball is approaching at chest level or above, let it go past you. Chances are it will rebound off the back wall, and you'll have a good set up. Don't follow such a shot into back court. Whenever possible, let the ball come to you.

Now what if the ball is coming at you between waist and chest level? *If* you're in a good position for a full stroke, return it before it hits the back wall. If you're not, you'll probably have another chance, because this ball is almost certain to bounce once, then strike the back wall and rebound.

If the ball is approaching the back wall below waist level, you'd better run and return it even if you don't have time to set up properly. This ball may die just before or just after touching the back wall.

If you've decided to play the ball off the back wall, try to judge the speed at which it's traveling. If it's going slowly, it may rebound only about three feet toward center court. After you've made this judgment, move into striking range, then let the ball pass you on its way to the front wall. Hitting the ball from behind lets you take advantage of its momentum.

This forward momentum should make these balls among the easiest ones to play. You don't have reverse their direction as you do with most shots. All you have to do is add to their speed and aim them away from your opponent.

Don't let this seeming simplicity fool you, however. To get the most out of back wall play, you're going to have to get into position and use your best forehand stroke. Your goal during your practice sessions is learning *how* to get into the best possible position, and *when* to hit the ball.

Your first few practices should be without your racquet.

1. Hold the ball in your left hand, and stand halfway between the side walls and about five feet away from the back wall. Face the right side wall.

**2.** Toss the ball to the back wall with an underhand motion, and release it about head height. It should be thrown hard enough to make it rebound near your feet.

3. Let the ball bounce once on the floor. As it rises, start *sliding* your feet toward the front wall. This sliding motion is essential. Don't cross one foot over the other, or you may lose your balance.
4. When the ball is at knee level and in front of you, catch it with your left hand.

To get the most out of this practice, concentrate on the feel of sliding toward the front wall, while judging the speed and height of the ball. You'll have to watch the ball closely as it strikes the back wall, bounces, and reaches its peak, then starts its second descent to the floor. Do this drill again and again, until you can actually feel the rhythm of your body moving with the ball.

Don't throw the ball so hard that it flies past you before you can move naturally with it. And don't toss it so lightly that you only have to move a foot or two before you catch it. Remember that what you have to learn is the *movement* of getting into position, not just when to catch the ball. This motion is the winning technique of back wall play.

Make sure that you slide smoothly, and that your knees are loose and slightly bent. Don't start your sliding motion until the ball rebounds near your feet. When you catch the ball, your whole body should be in the same position it would be in if you were executing a forehand stroke.

Now continue with your practice, using your racquet. As you begin your stroke, face the side wall. During your follow-through, pivot toward the front wall. This turning and pivoting will add speed and power to your stroke.

In this practice, the ball should hit the front wall at about the same height as it was at contact point, so don't tilt the racquet head. Hit the ball hard enough so that it rebounds off the front

**Waiting for the ball to rebound.**

wall and travels back and past you. Aim at a point on the front wall that will allow the ball to return about an arm's length away from you.

See how well you can control the ball? It's your hours of practice that have given you that control.

Double check the following points to get the most out of your practice.

1. Do I keep my balance at all times? (The sliding motion will help you to do this.)
2. Is the ball in front of me and at knee height when I hit it?
3. Was my wrist cocked as I started my stroke? Did I uncock it at contact point?
4. Did I start out close enough to the back wall to actually follow the ball toward center court? In actual play, it may not always be convenient to retreat into back court, but if you don't, you may find yourself reaching backward and executing a weak, flicking type of stroke.

One final important note—while you're doing all this gliding and reading of the ball, don't forget to keep one eye on your opponent. Only then will you know where to place your return shot.

When you've mastered the basic movements of back wall play, work on kills, passes, and ceiling balls, using back wall rebounds. The more variety you have, the more you can keep your opponent on the defensive. Use a pinch shot when he's in the back court, and another type of kill when he's in center or front court.

Ron Rubenstein offers this advice. "I use the kill about 75% of the time when I get my backhand shot off the back wall. I try not to kill when my opponent is in front court, however."

## Back Corner Play

One of the most important keys to winning play is becoming a good back corner player. Most of your opponents, if they're smart, will aim most of their passes, and *all* of their serves, to the back corners. It takes time to learn the skills of back corner play,

**A good back-corner shot.**

so don't become discouraged if you're having a problem with it.

Reading the ball is the important thing here. And to be able to read the ball requires hours of practice. If you're not willing to spend that time, your only hope will be that your opponent can't aim the ball very well. But you shouldn't count on that. It's true that it's hard for even an expert to land a ball in a back corner for an outright ace. It's true, also, that near misses are nearly as effective in corner shots as the ones that are 100% perfect.

The ball can "freak," or rebound in what may seem to be a totally unexpected path. It may suddenly die while you're trying to make an instant decision. You may be lucky to be able to dig the ball out of the corner with only a foot of room in which to make your stroke.

But even with these difficult shots, there are ways to improve your chances. First of all, be prepared for them, because all good opponents will aim for the corners. Take the ready

position halfway between the side walls. React as soon as you see that it's going to be a corner ball. With your knees bent and your racquet at chest level, run and get in position. As soon as possible, decide just how and where the ball will angle out of the corner, then use as full a stroke as possible.

Your chances are often better if you aim the ball toward the ceiling, using a wrist snap.

You'll probably never be entirely happy with your back corner play. It's one of those situations where you'll just have to do the best you can under the circumstances. Perhaps you'll just decide to let it die. But if you can possibly get into position, a weak return is usually better than none at all. The longer you can keep the rally going, the better chance you'll have to force your opponent into back corner play. At that time, you'll be able to even things up.

## Side Wall-Back Wall Corner Return

This return is the most common, and unfortunately, the most difficult back corner ball you'll have to deal with. First it bounces on the floor, then it strikes the side wall, travels to the back wall, and rebounds onto the floor again. You're going to have to deal with all of the changes in angles and directions the ball will take as it bounces around.

The angles will change with each shot, depending on how hard the ball was hit, on where your opponent was standing when he hit it, and how close it was to the back wall when it hit the side wall.

Of course, reading the ball is the answer. That ability comes from experience, but you can increase your chances of returning the shot if you practice some techniques.

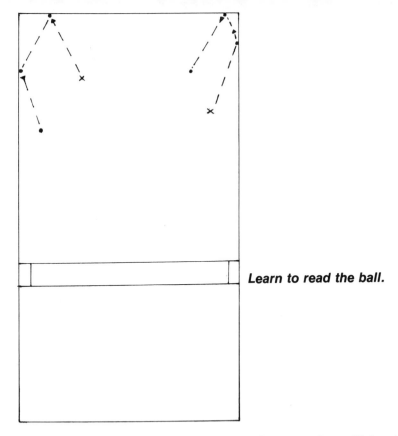

**Learn to read the ball.**

As with back wall play, your first practice will be done without your racquet.

1. Stand near the right back corner (if you're right-handed). With your left hand, toss the ball against the right side wall with an underhand motion. Angle the ball so that it will rebound toward the back wall. Use enough force so that, after rebounding, it will come out well into the back court area.

2. Use the same sliding motion that you used in your back wall practice. Move toward the opposite side wall, traveling with the ball as it angles off the back wall.

3. Let the ball pass you and bounce on the floor.

**4.** When it has descended to the proper contact point (knee level) catch it with your left hand.

The harder the ball strikes the side wall, the sooner it will rebound into your range. Be prepared to start sliding or you won't be able to catch it.

During these exercises, don't turn your back to the front wall. Get into the habit of standing sideways in relation to it, because that's the best position from which to hit the ball. While you're sliding, your back should be toward the opposite side wall.

Do this drill again and again, throwing the ball from different angles and at different heights. Notice what the ball does each time.

Now do the drill while using your racquet. Pivot during your stroke to give it more power. Your follow-through should leave you facing the front wall, ready for your opponent's return.

After you have that down, start returning the ball *before* it bounces. This skill is an advanced one, but the sooner you start to learn it the better. In real court play, the ball may die after it bounces, so you're going to have to hit it as soon as possible.

## Back Wall-Side Wall Corner Return

In these shots, the ball will bounce on the floor, strike the back wall, then rebound off the side wall. It's an easier shot to handle than the side wall-back wall return, because it will be angling toward the front wall. If you give it a push in the right direction, you'll have a good shot.

To practice this return, toss the ball into the back wall, but angle it so it will rebound off the right side wall. Slide toward the opposite side wall, and wait for the proper contact point. Aim the ball away from an imaginary opponent and toward the front wall.

Now you should practice both of these returns with your backhand. Your opponent is going to force you to use the left corner as much as possible. In every case, judge as soon as possible whether the ball is going to come off the back wall or the side wall, then figure the speed and the angle it will take. Slide to the proper return area, and wait for the knee level contact point before you hit the ball.

## Side Wall Play

The ball is heading toward the side wall near center court. What should you, as the receiver, be prepared to do?

First, you should quickly decide just how and where the ball will angle off the wall. Next, you should decide whether to let the ball come to you, or whether you should go to it.

Most beginners, who haven't developed the wisdom and the patience to wait for the ball, will automatically run after the ball. They will crowd it, cut short their stroke, and hit it too soon. They may even miss the ball entirely, because they didn't take into account the angle it would take.

An experienced player knows that a good, lively ball will almost always head into center court after only slightly touching the side wall. They figure out the angle of the rebound, move into position, and wait.

If you want to be an expert, you'll do as the pros do. Be prepared to change your position slightly if you read the ball wrong. As you wait, face the side wall, but angle yourself toward the front wall, and keep your knees slightly bent.

*A strong forehand shot close to the wall.*

If you see that the ball is going to continue to hug the side wall, move toward it, and set up. Don't worry about the fact that there's a wall a couple of feet away from you. If you're too aware of it, you'll end up chopping at the ball and forgetting about where your opponent is. Use a good, full, strong stroke as if you were in center court. The only difference will be that you have to clear the wall. By not letting the wall bother you, you can *scrape* the ball away from it, and stay in the rally.

Remember that the time to perfect any technique is during your practice sessions, not in the excitement of competition. Every trick you learn will build your confidence. And every match you win by using those tricks will build your confidence even more. Many baseball players will never be able to hit a home run, no matter how hard they try. Almost anyone can be a home-run king on a racquetball court.

Have you tried to talk your parents into joining you in a racquetball game lately? If you place your shots accurately, you can compete with them as equals. Make them run after the balls, get them winded, then wind up the rally with a kill. They may be bigger and stronger than you, but *you've* been practicing.

**Scraping the ball off the wall.**

# 9

# *Strategy*

Backhand strokes, ceiling shots, the rules of racquetball—all of these can be learned by study and practice. Successful strategy—a winning battle plan—is not acquired so easily. It can be developed only over a long period of time and by playing in a lot of competitions. You have to observe, to test, and to discover the style of play that's right for you.

You almost have to develop a sixth sense that takes over when there's no time to think. This sixth sense isn't anything mysterious. It happens when you can read the ball, when you can predict what your opponent is going to do, and when you're confident enough in your own ability to trust your instincts.

A good battle plan is made up of many things. It consists of knowing how and when to play offensively and defensively. It means playing one way when you're winning and another when you're losing. It means being able to slow down or to speed up the rally so you can control the game. And your battle plan must be flexible enough to change as the situation changes.

It's possible to learn all that you need to know about competitive play and about strategy just by doing the actual playing. However, if you want to speed up the process, find a pro or a coach and take some lessons. Build your strategy around your skills, while continuing to improve that sloppy back wall play, or your weak pinch shot.

There are some general strategy rules that have worked for so many expert players that they are worth studying. Maybe you can put some of them to work for you.

1. A racquetball game seldom lasts more than thirty minutes, so you're going to have to be alert and warmed up before you enter the court. Always do your warm up and stretching exercises to get your muscles and your mind ready to go.

    If you're playing a serious game, try to get your opponent to play a short pre-game warm-up session with you. Use this time to test him and to see what shots cause him the most trouble. Many of your opponents won't take the trouble to study *you*, so you'll be one up on them before you start.

2. Remember that the player who controls center court controls the rally.

3. Make your opponent play the kind of game *you* like to play. If he's a "blaster" who specializes in kills and power drives, send him lobs or medium speed Z shots. Those will make him return the ball at shoulder height. The more you can frustrate him, the more likely he is to make mistakes.

    On the other hand, if he tries the same technique on you, try to kill the ball with a drop shot.

4. Never underestimate the importance of the serve. You can afford to gamble with your opening serve. Use a risky, daring type of shot to confuse and surprise your opponent. However, if you've committed a fault, be a little more cautious. Hang on to that serve as long as you can.

5. Know where your opponent is at all times. Charlie Brumfield says, "If I'm having any success in controlling a rally, I know exactly where my opponent is. And if I can get him retrieving in the left or right back corners of the court, I know he can't recover quickly enough to regain center court before I hit my next shot. Then it's just a matter of hitting the ball to the side of the court opposite from where he's standing."

6. When your opponent is attempting a shot, always stand where he can see you. You can't physically prevent him from making that shot, but you can put mental pressure on him by letting him know that you're ready to pounce on his slightest mistake. Act confident, even if you don't feel that way.

   You can also position yourself to cut down on his choice of shots. Stand a few feet in front of him and between him and the far side wall. The only shots he'll be able to safely make are to the near side wall or to the front wall. The more you can limit his choice, the more you'll know what's coming up.

7. If you're in the lead, don't gamble or change your game plan. After all, you must already be doing the right things. If you're trailing, try some of your riskier shots. You've got everything to gain and not much to lose. Remember that the game can turn around at any point.

An important part of any strategy is knowing when to use a particular type of shot. Your decision should be based on two things.

First, can you aim a certain shot accurately from where you're standing? You may attempt a kill and succeed when you're using your forehand from center court. If you're using your backhand, though, you may have to be in front court to get the same result.

Second, how good is your opponent? You can learn the answer to this question by watching him in the pre-game warm-ups.

In general, you can use more daring returns when you're in control of center court. Attack the ball, cut off passes, and make your opponent run. If he manages to move up to center court, use a drop shot aimed at the side wall furthest from him. Try a down the wall pass to get him into back court. For a change of pace, use your Z shot.

If your opponent is behind the receiving line and you're in front court, use a straight kill. A pinch shot is good here also. Just make sure the ball angles away from him.

Save your defensive play for the times when you've been driven into back court. Now's the time for your ceiling balls. Wait for him to make a mistake that lets you play a ball off the back wall, then react quickly with a pass or a kill. As soon as you're back in center court, go back to your offensive style of play.

But what if the game goes sour no matter what you do? You're trailing 10-0, and becoming frustrated and angry. *Don't give up!* A racquetball game can change directions on the basis of one good shot. You can still regain the serve, turn the game around, and come out on top.

On the other hand, if you're the one who's leading, *don't get over-confident* and start to slack off. Keep playing hard, steadily, and with your over all strategy in mind.

Randy Stafford, who is a racquetball expert, once played

a particularly tough competition. Afterward, he talked about how he won. "It wasn't just a good serve or a ceiling ball that won the match. Thoughtful strategy and the composure needed to carry it out were just as important."

You'll never know whether or not you can return a ball unless you try. Remember, however, that you are going to miss some, and it's not the end of the world if you do. Get back into your ready position and be prepared for the next one.

Having a good strategy and making it work requires that you become a skilled player. But winning is more than skills. It's a state of mind. Keep a cool head, have faith in yourself, and think positively. With attitudes like that, you *can't* be a loser.

# Doubles

"How about a game of doubles?" If you like racquetball and you like being with a group of friends, you won't be able to pass up an invitation like that.

Besides a lot of fun, doubles offers a special sort of challenge. Instead of having only one opponent, you'll have two of them, each waiting to smash the ball back to you. Whenever you make a decision, you'll have to consider your partner. There will be four people on the court, and thus twice the number of moving arms, legs, and racquets. The action in center court is fast and furious, and your reflexes are going to have to be *sharp*.

Doubles can be confusing, and even dangerous, unless every player is extra careful.

In some ways, though, doubles play is easier than singles. Your partner's strengths can make up for your weaknesses. Since you're covering only half the court, you can spend more time setting up and less time running. Doubles has been called a "thinking persons's game." If you and your partner can play well together, the total ability of your team may be more than your individual abilities.

**Doubles partners.**

If you just want to have a good time, you can play your doubles game with anyone. But if you're playing a serious competition, there are some important things to consider before you pick a partner, or before someone picks you for his team.

Doubles partners should complement each other. If one is a good kill shot player, the other should be a good "set up artist," who can place shots to get the other team out of position. If one partner has a good forehand, the other should have a good backhand. If one is a powerful, aggressive player, the other should be a good defense and back wall player.

Neither partner should want to hog the limelight. Any victory should be earned and shared equally. If there's a defeat, it shouldn't be followed by name calling and fault finding.

Doubles is played basically the same way as singles. The main difference is that your strategy and choice of shots have to be decided with three other people in mind. You and your partner must talk everything over with each other. Before the game, discuss each other's strengths and weaknesses and individual types of play. You can't be close minded as you talk about strategy.

Don't be like some players who end up acting as if their *partners* are their opponents.

Decide upon a system of short, clear signals that can be used during the game. They should be as uncomplicated as possible, such as calling out "Yours," or "Mine," if there's a question as to who should return the ball.

In competitive play, each team is allowed three time outs during a game. They are thirty to sixty seconds long. Use this time to update your battle plan according to the changing situation. Iron out any misunderstandings that may have occurred in the heat of the play.

The most commonly used team formation is the half-and-half. Each player stands on his side of an imaginary line that divides the court in half from front to back. This formation works especially well when one partner has a strong backhand, or is left handed. That partner can play on the left hand side of the court.

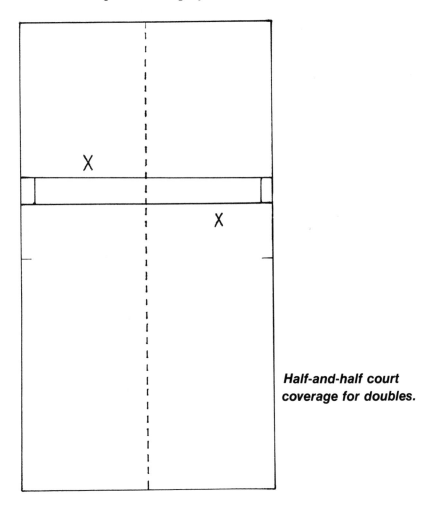

*Half-and-half court coverage for doubles.*

Some players like the "I" position. Here, the more aggressive and faster player works in the front court so he can use his kill shots and react to the other team's kill attempts. The more defensive and deliberate player stands in back court where he can use his ceiling and pass shots. If he's also a good back wall player, this combination can be a real winner.

In any formation, each partner should be ready to run to any part of the court if his partner gets out of position.

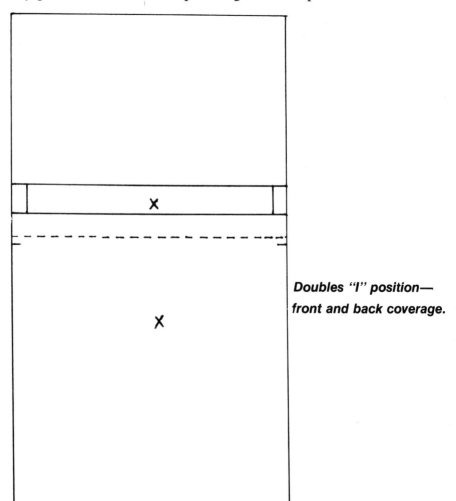

*Doubles "I" position—*
*front and back coverage.*

When a team first gets the serve, only one partner is allowed to serve. If he loses the serve, the team is out. During the rest of the game, both partners are allowed to serve before the team is out.

During the serve, the server stands in the same place he stands in during singles play. His partner stands in the service box until after the ball has passed the short line.

Either player on the receiving team can return the ball. If both of them swing at the ball at the same time, there's no penalty. But only one of them can actually hit it. After the return, if the team is using the half-and-half formation, both receivers should advance to six or eight feet back of the short line and across from each other.

If the receivers are using the "I" formation, the stronger partner should move to front court as soon as possible.

Here are some suggestions for winning doubles play.
1. You may have to use shorter strokes in center court if it becomes crowded. Use your longer, more powerful strokes in back court.
2. *Control center court.* This position is even more important in doubles play. Here you can more easily keep an eye on the ball and use your kills.
3. Kill shots are essential to a winning doubles game. Vary your pattern of play by varying your type of kill.
4. *Keep your eye on the ball.* If your partner is out of position, or attempts to hit the ball and misses, you should be ready to jump in and save the day.
5. In general, the more the members of a team stay away from each other, the better their court coverage will be.

**6.** Use the isolation strategy. If one of your opponents is a better player than the other, or if one of them is having a hot streak, and he can't do anything wrong, signal to your partner to play the ball to the weaker player. When the stronger partner has dropped out of position to help him, or when he's dropped his guard, surprise him with a hard drive angled toward his backhand side.

**7.** All doubles players must be especially aware of the need for safety and consideration. Stay out of each other's way and give the other team clear paths to the front wall. If there's danger of hitting someone with your racquet, stop your swing and replay the point.

## Basic Doubles Shots

Accuracy is perhaps more important in doubles than in singles because there are twice as many people on the court to avoid hitting with the ball. You can still combine power with that accuracy if you plan your strategy with safety in mind. A winning game doesn't mean that someone has to get hurt.

### Doubles Serves

Avoid serving low drives or medium lobs into the back corner behind your partner. The chances are too high that as he moves out of the service box, he'll be hit with the serve return. A poorly hit lob serve will also tempt your opponents to return it on the fly, another shot that will be dangerously close to your partner.

Z serves and high lobs are better choices in most cases.

Carefully placed power drives can be used to break up the pattern of play.

### Doubles Serve Returns

The type of return will, of course, depend on the type of serve. The object remains the same as in singles—to drive the opposing team out of center court.

It's usually a mistake to try to kill the ball on a serve return, because both opponents will be in front of you. Unless the kill is a rollout, one of them will get to it easily and quickly.

If the serve is weak, your best bet is to use a cross-court shot. The angle of this shot should be wide enough to avoid hitting your opponent. A good target point is the side wall just behind where an opponent is standing.

Z shots and ceiling shots are effective in driving your opponents to the back court. A strong serve should usually be returned with a ceiling shot, because if you try a pass and it's not successful, one of your opponents will have a good set up in center court.

# The Rally

Effective kills are *essential* in doubles play, and most of your points will be made by using them. Passes are good only if your opponents are out of position.

Kills must be especially well executed if they're going to succeed. If you can hit a good pinch shot, use it when you see that an opponent is getting tired or is out of position to return it. After you shoot a few pinches and he's in position for another, switch to a wide angled shot, such as a V pass.

If the ball approaches at waist level or below, don't let it go past you to the back wall. This general rule is as important in doubles as it is in singles. If you're in center court and your opponents are behind you, you may be able to kill the ball even when you're forced to use a higher contact point than usual. On the other hand, if you let a waist level ball go by, your opponents will be able to advance to center court as you follow the ball to the back wall. At that time, your kill will have to be a rollout to be a winner.

The overhead drive and the overhead kill are effective weapons in doubles play. Since the motions of the stroke may make your opponents think that you're preparing for a ceiling shot, you can catch them off guard.

To hit an overhead shot, the ball must, of course, be approaching at above head level. Use the kill to make your opponent run from back court to front court. Use the drive if you want to make him return the ball at chest level. That will be a hard shot for him, and he'll be forced to return it defensively.

These shots are needed when it looks as if the game is going to turn into a long, dull ceiling ball rally. Save those ceiling balls for when your opponents are in center court, and you don't want to risk a pass or a kill.

If you don't have enough people to get up a doubles game, you can get two friends and play a rousing game of "cutthroat." The rules are simple. One player has the serve and competes against the other two. He continues to score points until he loses a rally. At that time, another player gets the serving position.

Each player keeps his own score. The game is over when someone gets 21 points.

How about you and your brother or sister or a friend getting into a doubles game with your mother and father? Or here's another good idea—rent a couple of racquetball courts for your next birthday party. Tell everyone to dress up in their best T-shirts and cut-offs and to be prepared for an active afternoon. There's nothing like a good fast game to get your guests over those party jitters. Later, when they come to your house for refreshments, everyone will be relaxed and you'll all have plenty to talk about.

# Championship Attitudes

Playing good racquetball is much more than chasing the ball around the court. It's more than knowing the right shots, and controlling center court. It's more than having a strong, dependable backhand, or a well thought-out and executed strategy.

To be a *real* champion, you'll need the right mental attitude toward the game and toward other players. Attitudes deal with how you feel and think about things and people.

What do right attitudes have to do with winning a competition? For one thing, they give you the willpower to train and to stay in top physical condition. It takes willpower to get the right amount of sleep every night, when you'd much rather watch the late show on television. It takes willpower to pass up those potato chips and chocolate bars in favor of an apple or a salad.

Being a winner takes sacrifice, sometimes a lot of it. But if you're tired and poorly nourished, you're not going to have much of a chance against someone who's alert and healthy. Even if you just want to play for the fun of it, and most people do, you'll get a lot more enjoyment if you're not puffing and panting after five minutes of court time.

Steve Keeley, the 1971 National Champion, runs to keep in shape. "If you have time only to run or play racquetball," he advises, "then by all means play. But without running to keep in shape, you'll never have the power that will win you crucial matches."

The better your physical condition, the more self confidence you'll have. Self confidence is important to get good results in *anything*. And you can't be confident only when things are going your way. Anyone can do that. You also have to be confident when you're five points behind.

Marty Hogan, who became the 1978 Singles Champion, tried to win the national championship for several years. He didn't give up and as a result, he reached his goal. He has played racquetball since he was eight years old, and every time he had a chance he watched the top professional players in action. He knew how good they were when he started to enter competitions, but that didn't discourage him.

". . .I saw how good the top players were," he said. "But I know what my ability is, and I knew I could be the best. My best shot is my game. I can hit the ball from any position harder than anyone else."

Hard work, plus self confidence—they go hand in hand on the road to success. The effect that this combination has on winning has been proved again and again. When two nearly equal players compete, the one who comes out on top is the one who has the most confidence. He's the one who has practiced so long and so hard that he *knows* he couldn't be better prepared.

What if you've prepared, but you know you'll still lie awake tossing and turning on the night before a big match? Read a book, watch television, or take a hot bath so you can relax. Think of all the hours of practice you've put in. Tell yourself that you're ready for the match, and then get some sleep.

Useless worry isn't the same as the natural nervousness that comes before a big game. That nervousness is just your body's way of "psyching" you up and getting you ready to compete. It will make it possible for you to think and act quickly, to make smashing serves, and to out-play your opponent.

And remember that no one wins *every* game. The important thing is to give every shot your best effort, play consistently, and keep a cool head. If you play like a champion, you'll be a champion, whether you win or lose.

Good attitudes go a long way beyond keeping yourself healthy and playing a good game. Racquetball calls for players who are honest, and grown up enough to admit that they really could have avoided that hinder. It calls for people who can follow the unwritten rules of the game, as well as those that appear in the official handbook. As you become a better player, you should become a better person also.

It's against the unwritten rules to disturb your opponent's concentration by making loud, rude, or unusual noises while he's trying to make a shot; to lose your temper; to argue with other players or with a referee in a tournament; or to walk off the court and sulk when things don't go your way.

If you strongly disagree with someone's opinion of the

legality of your shot, stop the game and discuss the matter calmly. Maybe you won't be able to change his mind, but the more grown up you act, the more chance you'll have to convince him. Often, the best thing to do is to play the point over. This is a good solution in the case of a hinder, because it's often hard to decide whether it was avoidable or not.

Playing a safe game is also part of the unwritten rules. Every player is going to get hit with the ball now and then.

Someone can also get in the way of a swinging racquet, but that
shouldn't happen often. Consideration and common sense will
cut way down on the number of such occurrences. If your opponent keeps getting too close, or crowding you, there are better
ways of letting him know about it than by socking him with your
racquet. Ask him to move. If that doesn't work, stop your swing
and call a safety hinder. If you do this enough times, he'll get the
idea.

Honesty comes high on the list of unwritten rules. Imagine, for a moment, that you're playing a tie breaker in an important match and you're three points behind. The ball bounces for a second time before you return it. You know that your shot was illegal, but since you were so close to the back corner, no one else saw that second bounce. The referee says nothing. You could keep your mouth shut and win the point or the serve. It makes good sense to keep on playing. Right?

Wrong! You're breaking one of racquetball's most important unwritten rules—calling a point against yourself when you know something that no one else does. It's a hard rule to follow when you desperately need a point, but what's the good of winning when you know you did it dishonestly? If you have to cheat to win, how can you prove to yourself that you could have won honestly? There will always be that doubt in your mind, and your victory won't mean much.

Honesty works to your advantage in other ways also. Your good example of calling an illegal shot on yourself will make your opponent much more likely to be honest when he's in such a situation.

*You* can help to make racquetball the kind of game it should be. It should be based on fair play, sportsmanship, and respect for other players. The competition should be a friendly one. Following this simple rule takes the despair out of losing, and adds joy to the winning.

# ⑫

# *Meet Some Racquetball Champions*

# Jerry Zuckerman

In his first year on the pro tour, Jerry Zuckerman moved into the number thirteen spot. In 1977, he won both the IRA and National Racquetball Club (NRC) National Open Championships, and was recently named the IRA Player of the Year.

Jerry is a leftie who has a powerful forehand, and plays consistently well.

# Mike Yellen

Mike Yellen earned a place among racquetball's top competitors during his first six months on the pro tour. He was the youngest player on the tour, but amazed everyone by winning the Montreal Pro-Am, and by ranking high in the International Professional Racquetball Organization and the NRC 1978 National Championships.

# Jennifer Harding

Jennifer Harding is currently in the No. 2 spot on the women's pro racquetball tour. She started playing racquetball in 1972 and now gives it all of her time.

"It's the life of Reilly for me," she says. "I love it. Racquetball is the ideal sport for women. Handball is too rough on the hands and most people, including women, want more excitement and competition than they can find in jogging. Also, a woman can compete with a man much more easily in racquetball."

Jennifer proved that racquetball is an equalizer among people of different strengths and sizes. After winning regional tournaments for three years in a row, she couldn't find any other women who could compete with her. "So I started entering men's tournaments," she recalls.

Her drive serves to both sides of the court, and her powerful, accurate forehand gives both the men and women opponents a run for their money.

# Rita Hoff

Rita Hoff is called one of the finest pro players in the world, male or female.. Recently she whipped two pro football stars in succession on the racquetball court.

In 1978, she reached the semi-final round of the Los Angeles Pro-Am, and the quarter finals in the national championships. Her goal is to become the best female player in the United States.

# Alicia Moore

In 1977, Alicia Moore won every Pro-Am in the Western United States, and in 1978 she went on to win the NRC National Ladies Amateur Championship. She is now thinking about turning pro.

Up to this point, Alicia admits that she didn't have to work too hard to win because she has so much natural ability. She knows that if she turns pro, she's going to have to put a lot more effort into her game.

"I plan to commit myself totally," she says. "I want to give myself the chance to see what my full potential really is."

That winning attitude along with her winning form will get her to the top.

# Jeff Bowman

In spite of not having entered a tournament for the entire previous year, Jeff Bowman won the 1978 NRC Men's Singles Championship. His strong serve and expert forehand will continue to keep him at the top.

# Jerry Hilecher

Jerry Hilecher's father taught him how to play racquetball 14 years ago. "At first I was the worst," he says, "but then my Dad bought me a couple of aluminum racquets, and all of a sudden I got a lot better." By the time he was 15, he was the city champion of St. Louis, Missouri.

It wasn't just the type of racquet that let him reach five of the nine semi-finals of the NRC pro tournaments, and to become the fourth-ranked player on the pro circuit. It's Jerry's love for the game.

"There's fast action, impossible dives for the shots," he states enthusiastically, "and players just really going for it 100 percent of the time."

Jerry also has the ability to "psych out" his opponent. "Professional racquetball is as much of a psychological game as a physical one," he says. "And the energy of the audience gets me up."

# Martha McDonald

Martha McDonald has been called ". . .the most rapidly improving and singly dangerous player on tour."

It has also been said of her: "Martha has better potential and better skills than any other woman in the country. She's a world class athlete."

Martha learned how to play racquetball on a three-wall outdoor court, and is now ranked as the No. 7 women's pro player in the United States. She is considered the fastest player on the women's tour, and plays with an unusual quick-wrist style. She has the ability to shoot almost any ball out of the air.

# Marci Greer

Marci Greer ranks No. 14 on the women's pro tour, and her fellow pros rave about her. Jennifer Harding said that Marci's performance was "the toughest match I had before I reached the finals. Every time I draw Marci, I know I have my work cut out for me."

Marci plays a powerful game. To stay in shape she runs five miles every day.

# Thirty-Minute Practice Schedule

If you were a sports pro, you'd probably be practicing several hours a day almost every day of the year. At this point, you're more than likely just interested in having a good time on the racquetball court, but you may want to improve your skills so you can have a better time. Here's a practice schedule that you can follow once or twice a week, or more often if you want to. It will help you get the most out of the time you spend in your racquetball sessions.

| Shots | Number of Times | Area of Court to Practice From |
|---|---|---|
| Ceiling Ball | 30 | Back |
| Z Ball | 5 | All Areas |
| Straight Kill | 10 | Center and Back |
| Pinch | 10 | All Areas |
| Front Wall-Side Wall Kill | 10 | Center and Back |
| Drop Shot | 10 | Front |
| Down-the-Wall Pass | 15 | All Areas |
| V Pass | 10 | All Areas |
| Overhead Kill | 10 | Center and Back |
| Overhead Drive | 10 | Center and Back |
| Cross-Court Pass | 5 | Center Court |
| Lob Serve | 10 | Service Zone |
| Power Drive | 10 | Service Zone |

If you're having trouble with a particular shot, skip one or two of the others and concentrate on that. Change this schedule to fit your own needs.

# Summary of Rules

## The Game

1. Racquetball may be played by two, three, or four players. When played by two, it's called singles; by three, cutthroat; by four, doubles.
2. It is played with a racquet and a ball in a three or four-walled court.
3. The object is to win each rally by serving or by returning the ball so the opponent is unable to send it back to you.
4. A rally is over when a side is not able to return the ball before it touches the floor twice.
5. The serving side wins a point when it serves an ace, or when it wins the rally. When it loses the rally, it loses the serve.
6. The first side to earn 21 points wins the game.
7. A match is won by the first side to win two out of three games.

## Serving Rules

1. The first serve is decided by the toss of a coin.
2. Before each serve, the server should call out the score, giving his score first.
3. The server may stand in any part of the service zone during his serve. He may step on the line, but no part of his foot may extend behind the line of the service zone. He must remain inside the service zone until the ball has passed the short line.
4. Serves may not be made until the opponent is ready to receive the ball.
5. In doubles play, the partner who serves the initial serve must serve first throughout the game. He is the only one who serves during the initial service, which

is the first serve of the game. If he loses that serve, the team is out. After the initial serve, both serving partners will serve.

6. In doubles, if the members of the serving side serve in the wrong order, or if the same player serves two succeeding serves, they lose the serve.

7. In doubles, the server's partner must remain in the service box. He may not leave it until the served ball has crossed the short line.

## Dead Ball Serves

A dead ball results in the replay of a point. They occur when:

1. The served ball hits the server's doubles partner as he stands in the service box.

2. The served ball passes too close to the server or his doubles partner, so that the receiver cannot see it. This is known as a "screen ball." Any serve passing behind the server's doubles partner as he stands in the service box is a screen ball.

## Fault Serves

Two faults in succession result in loss of the serve. Faults occur when:

1. The server leaves the service zone before the ball passes the short line.

2. The server's doubles partner leaves the service box before the served ball passes the short line.

3. The served ball rebounds off the front wall, then hits the floor in front of the short line.

4. The served ball rebounds off the front wall and hits both side walls without touching the floor in between them.

5. A served ball touches the ceiling.

6. A served ball hits the back wall without first touching the floor.

7. A served ball leaves the court.

## Out Serves

A server is out when:

1. The server bounces the ball more than three times before attempting his serve. Accidental dropping of the ball counts as a bounce.
2. Any attempt to strike the ball which results in a miss.
3. The ball touches any part of the server's body.
4. The served ball strikes the server's partner, the floor, or the side wall before striking the front wall.
5. The served ball touches the server's body on the rebound, or the served ball touches the server's doubles partner after he has stepped out of the service box.
6. The served ball hits the crotch between the front wall and the floor.

## Serve Return Rules

Failure to follow these rules results in a point for the server.

1. The server must stand at least five feet behind the short line as he waits for the serve.
2. He cannot return the ball until it passes the short line.
3. The ball must be returned to the front wall without touching the floor. Hitting the crotch between the front wall and the floor is considered the same as hitting the floor. The ball may touch any other playing surface, or combination of playing surfaces, before it touches the front wall.
4. No part of the receiver's body may cross the short line before he makes the return.
5. Any failure to return the ball before it touches the floor twice results in a point for the server.

## Changes of Serve

A player shall continue serving until:

1. He makes an out serve.
2. He commits two faults in succession.

**3.** He hits his doubles partner with the ball, unless the ball is rebounding from the floor.

**4.** He fails to return the ball.

**5.** He commits an avoidable hinder.

When the player loses the serve, he and the receiver switch places.

## The Rally

**1.** If the server switches hands to hit the ball, he is out. If the receiver switches hands, the server gets a point.

## Hinders

The ball becomes dead and the point will be replayed when:

**1.** Your returned ball hits an opponent before it strikes the front wall.

**2.** When you've accidentally blocked your opponent's view of the ball.

**3.** When you've accidentally blocked your opponent's path to the front wall.

If the server commits one of the following hinders, he is out. If the receiver commits one, the server gets a point.

**1.** Deliberate failure to move to give the opponent a clear path to the front wall.

**2.** Deliberately moving between the opponent and the ball, so as to block the opponent's view.

**3.** Deliberately moving into the path of the moving ball.

**4.** Deliberately pushing an opponent.

All hinder calls must be made immediately.

# Glossary

**Ace:** A serve that bounces twice before the receiver can return it.

**Avoidable hinder:** A blocking or interference that could have been prevented.

**Back court:** The area from the short line to the back wall.

**Backhand:** A basic stroke that is played from the left side by right-handers, and the right side by left-handers.

**Ceiling ball:** A shot that hits the ceiling, front wall, and floor, then rebounds to the back court.

**Center court:** The area between the service line and back court.

**Contact point:** The point at which the racquet and ball meet.

**Cross-court shot:** A ball that travels from one side of the court to the other after hitting the front wall.

**Crotch:** Where two playing surfaces join.

**Crowding:** Playing too close to your opponent, or standing too close to the ball as you make your shot.

**Cutthroat:** A three-player game.

**Defensive shot:** A shot that is made to keep the player in the rally, not necessarily to win a point.

**Die:** A ball which stops after hitting the wall is said to have died.

**Doubles:** A four-player game.

**Drive:** A strong, straight shot.

**Drop shot:** A soft shot that dies after hitting the front wall.

**Fault:** An illegal serve.

**Fly ball:** A shot that is hit immediately after it hits the front wall.

**Follow-through:** The natural body movements that follow a stroke.

**Forehand:** A shot hit from the right for a right-hander, and on the left for a left-hander.

**Front court:** The area between the service line and the front wall.

**Front wall kill:** A shot that dies after hitting only the front wall.

**Front wall-Side wall kill:** A shot that dies after hitting the front wall, then rebounding off the side wall.

**Grip:** The way the racquet is held.

**Half-and-half:** In doubles, the division of the court lengthwise.

**Head:** The hitting area of the racquet.

**Hinder:** Blocking a player from his chance to see the ball or to safely make his shot.

**I Formation:** In doubles, when one player plays front court and the other plays back court.

**Kill shot:** A shot hit so low that it rebounds in a way that can't be returned.

**Lob serve:** A serve that hits the front wall high, then rebounds upward, landing in back court.

**Long serve:** A serve that hits the back wall without first hitting the floor.

**Match:** A set of three games.

**Offensive shot:** A shot whose main purpose is to win a point.

**Out:** The loss of serve.

**Overhead:** A stroke in which the arm moves up and over the head.

**Passing shot:** A shot designed to pass an opponent so he can't reach it.

**Pinch shot:** A shot that hits the front wall, then the side wall and dies. A tight front wall-side wall shot.

**Plum:** An easily returnable shot.

**Rally:** The exchange of shots between serves.

**Rollout:** An unreturnable kill shot.

**Screen:** Blocking an opponent's view of the ball.

**Serve:** Putting the ball into play.

**Set up:** Getting into position and range to make a shot.

**Short serve:** A serve that hits the floor before reaching the short line.

**Side wall-Front wall kill:** A kill that hits first the side wall, then the front wall.

**Singles:** A two-player game.

**Straight kill:** A kill shot that hits the front wall only.

**Three-wall serve:** A serve that hits the front wall and both side walls without touching the floor in between the side walls.

**Unavoidable hinder:** Unintentional or unpreventable interference of opponent's play.

**V pass:** A pass shot that rebounds in a wide V path.

**Wallpaper ball:** A shot that travels very close to the side wall on its way to back court.

**Z ball:** A shot that hits the front wall, side wall, and opposite side wall on the fly.

# Racquetball Associations

United States Racquetball Association (USRA)
>4101 Dempster St.
>Skokie, Il 60076
>(312) 673-4000
>President: Robert W. Kendler

National Racquetball Club (NRC)
>4101 Dempster St.
>Skokie, Il 60076
>(312) 673-4000
>President: Robert W. Kendler
>The National Racquetball Club is the professional arm of the United States Racquetball Association.

International Racquetball Association (IRA)
>5545 Murray Ave., Suite 202
>Memphis, Tenn. 38104
>(901) 274-2363

International Professional Racquetball Organization (IPRO)
>2714 Union Avenue Ext.
>Memphis, Tenn. 38112
>(901) 320-4248
>Business Manager: Dick Howard
>President: Bill Tanner

National Court Clubs Association (NCCA)
>423 Central Avenue
>Northfield, Il 60093
>(312) 446-5502
>Director: John S. Wineman, Jr.

# Some Racquetball Magazines

Racquetball Illustrated
    Bob Schultz, Editor
    CFW Enterprises
    7011 Sunset Blvd.
    Hollywood, CA 90028
    (213) 461-4324
    Bi-monthly circulation: 100,000

National Racquetball
    Chuck Leve, Editor
    4101 Dempster St.
    Skokie, Il 60076
    (312) 673-4000
    Official monthly publication of
    the USRA.
    Circulation: 65,000

Racquetball
    Luke St. Onge, Editor
    5545 Murray Ave., Suite 202
    Memphis, Tenn. 38104
    (901) 274-2363
    Official bi-monthly publication of
    the IRA.
    Circulation: 25,000

Racquetworld Review
    Tony Enyedy, Editor
    2340 Tampa Ave., Suite B
    El Cajon, CA 92020
    (714) 461-3210
    Circulation: 30,000 monthly

Racquet Magazine
    Gerald Jabara, Editor
    342 Madison Avenue
    New York, NY 10017
    (212) 687-2370
    Circulation: 75,000 bi-monthly